Three Crown Series

Arnold Apple:	Son of Guyana
J. P. Clark:	Three Plays
	Ozidi
J. C. de Graft:	Through a Film Darkly
	Sons and Daughters
R. Sarif Easmon:	Dear Parent and Ogre
Obi Egbuna:	Daughters of the Sun
Mbuyiseni Oswald Mtshali:	Sounds of a Cowhide Drum
Ola Rotimi:	The Gods are not to Blame
Wole Soyinka:	A Dance of the Forests
	The Lion and the Jewel
	Kongi's Harvest
	The Road
D. O. Umobuarie:	Black Justice
J. Wartemberg:	The Corpse's Comedy

Wole Soyinka

THE LION

and the

JEWEL

Oxford University Press

Oxford University Press, Walton Street, Oxford OX2 6DP

Oxford New York
Athens Auckland Bangkok Bogota Bombay
Buenos Aires Calcutta Cape Town Dar es Salaam
Delhi Florence Hong Kong Istanbul Karachi
Kuala Lumpur Madras Madrid Melbourne
Mexico City Nairobi Paris Singapore
Taipei Tokyo Toronto

and associated companies in
Berlin Ibadan

Oxford is a trade mark of Oxford University Press

ISBN 0 19 911083 2

First published 1962
Thirty-third impression 1996

Printed and bound in Hong Kong

Characters

SIDI the Village Belle

LAKUNLE School teacher

BAROKA the 'Bale' of Ilujinle

SADIKU His head wife

THE FAVOURITE

VILLAGE GIRLS

A WRESTLER

A SURVEYOR

SCHOOLBOYS

ATTENDANTS ON THE 'BALE'

Musicians, Dancers, Mummers,

Prisoners, Traders, the VILLAGE.

MORNING

A clearing on the edge of the market, dominated by an immense 'odan' tree. It is the village centre. The wall of the bush school flanks the stage on the right, and a rude window opens on to the stage from the wall. There is a chant of the 'Arithmetic Times' issuing from this window. It begins a short while before the action begins. Sidi enters from left, carrying a small pail of water on her head. She is a slim girl with plaited hair. A true village belle. She balances the pail on her head with accustomed ease. Around her is wrapped the familiar broad cloth which is folded just above her breasts, leaving the shoulders bare.

Almost as soon as she appears on the stage, the schoolmaster's face also appears at the window. (The chanting continues—'Three times two are six', 'Three times three are nine', etc.) The teacher Lakunle, disappears. He is replaced by two of his pupils, aged roughly eleven, who make a buzzing noise at Sidi, repeatedly clapping their hands across the mouth. Lakunle now re-appears below the window and makes for Sidi, stopping only to give the boys admonitory whacks on the head before they can duck. They vanish with a howl and he shuts the window on them. The chanting dies away. The schoolmaster is nearly twenty-three. He is dressed in an old-style English suit, threadbare but not ragged, clean but not ironed, obviously a size or two too small. His tie is done in a very small knot, disappearing beneath a shiny black waist-coat. He wears twenty-three-inch-bottom trousers, and blanco-white tennis shoes.

LAKUNLE: Let me take it.
SIDI: No.
LAKUNLE: Let me. [*Seizes the pail. Some water spills on him.*]
SIDI: [*delighted.*]
There. Wet for your pains.
Have you no shame?

LAKUNLE: That is what the stewpot said to the fire.
Have you no shame—at your age
Licking my bottom? But she was tickled
Just the same.
SIDI: The school teacher is full of stories
This morning. And now, if the lesson
Is over, may I have the pail?
LAKUNLE: No. I have told you not to carry loads
On your head. But you are as stubborn
As an illiterate goat. It is bad for the spine.
And it shortens your neck, so that very soon
You will have no neck at all. Do you wish to look
Squashed like my pupils' drawings?
SIDI: Why should that worry me? Haven't you sworn
That my looks do not affect your love?
Yesterday, dragging your knees in the dust
You said, Sidi, if you were crooked or fat,
And your skin was scaly like a . . .
LAKUNLE: Stop!
SIDI: I only repeat what you said.
LAKUNLE: Yes, and I will stand by every word I spoke.
But must you throw away your neck on that account?
Sidi, it is so unwomanly. Only spiders
Carry loads the way you do.
SIDI: [*huffily, exposing the neck to advantage.*]
Well, it is my neck, not your spider.
LAKUNLE: [*looks, and gets suddenly agitated.*]
And look at that! Look, look at that!
[*Makes a general sweep in the direction of her breasts.*]
Who was it talked of shame just now?
How often must I tell you, Sidi, that
A grown-up girl must cover up her . . .
Her . . . shoulders? I can see quite . . . quite
A good portion of—that! And so I imagine

Can every man in the village. Idlers
All of them, good-for-nothing shameless men
Casting their lustful eyes where
They have no business . . .

SIDI: Are you at that again? Why, I've done the fold
So high and so tight, I can hardly breathe.
And all because you keep at me so much.
I have to leave my arms so I can use them . . .
Or don't you know that?

LAKUNLE: You could wear something.
Most modest women do. But you, no.
You must run about naked in the streets.
Does it not worry you . . . the bad names,
The lewd jokes, the tongue-licking noises
Which girls, uncovered like you,
Draw after them?

SIDI: This is too much. Is it you, Lakunle,
Telling me that I make myself common talk?
When the whole world knows of the madman
Of Ilujinle, who calls himself a teacher!
Is it Sidi who makes the men choke
In their cups, or you, with your big loud words
And no meaning? You and your ragged books
Dragging your feet to every threshold
And rushing them out again as curses
Greet you instead of welcome. Is it Sidi
They call a fool—even the children—
Or you with your fine airs and little sense!

LAKUNLE: [*first indignant, then recovers composure.*]
For that, what is a jewel to pigs?
If now I am misunderstood by you
And your race of savages, I rise above taunts
And remain unruffled.

SIDI: [*furious, shakes both fists at him.*]

O . . . oh, you make me want to pulp your brain.

LAKUNLE: [*retreats a little, but puts her aside with a very lofty gesture.*]
A natural feeling, arising out of envy;
For, as a woman, you have a smaller brain
Than mine.

SIDI: [*madder still.*]
Again! I'd like to know
Just what gives you these thoughts
Of manly conceit.

LAKUNLE: [*very very, patronizing.*]
No, no. I have fallen for that trick before.
You can no longer draw me into arguments
Which go above your head.

SIDI: [*can't find the right words, chokes back.*]
Give me the pail now. And if you ever dare
To stop me in the streets again . . .

LAKUNLE: Now, now, Sidi . . .

SIDI: Give it or I'll . . .

LAKUNLE: [*holds on to her.*]
Please, don't be angry with me.
I didn't mean you in particular.
And anyway, it isn't what I say.
The scientists have proved it. It's in my books.
Women have a smaller brain than men
That's why they are called the weaker sex.

SIDI: [*throws him off.*]
The weaker sex, is it?
Is it a weaker breed who pounds the yam
Or bends all day to plant the millet
With a child strapped to her back?

LAKUNLE: That is all part of what I say.
But don't you worry. In a year or two
You will have machines which will do

Your pounding, which will grind your pepper
Without it getting in your eyes.

SIDI: O-oh. You really mean to turn
The whole world upside down.

LAKUNLE: The world? Oh, that. Well, maybe later.
Charity, they say, begins at home.
For now, it is this village I shall turn
Inside out. Beginning with that crafty rogue,
Your past master of self-indulgence—Baroka.

SIDI: Are you still on about the Bale?
What has he done to you?

LAKUNLE: He'll find out. Soon enough, I'll let him know.

SIDI: These thoughts of future wonders—do you buy them
Or merely go mad and dream of them?

LAKUNLE: A prophet has honour except
In his own home. Wise men have been called mad
Before me and after, many more shall be
So abused. But to answer you, the measure
Is not entirely of my own coinage.
What I boast is known in Lagos, that city
Of magic, in Badagry where Saro women bathe
In gold, even in smaller towns less than
Twelve miles from here . . .

SIDI: Well go there. Go to these places where
Women would understand you
If you told them of your plans with which
You oppress me daily. Do you not know
What name they give you here?
Have you lost shame completely that jeers
Pass you over.

LAKUNLE: No. I have told you no. Shame belongs
Only to the ignorant.

SIDI: Well, I am going.
Shall I take the pail or not?

LAKUNLE: Not till you swear to marry me.
[*Takes her hand, instantly soulful.*]
Sidi, a man must prepare to fight alone.
But it helps if he has a woman
To stand by him, a woman who . . .
Can understand . . . like you.

SIDI: I do?

LAKUNLE: Sidi, my love will open your mind
Like the chaste leaf in the morning, when
The sun first touches it.

SIDI: If you start that I will run away.
I had enough of that nonsense yesterday.

LAKUNLE: Nonsense? Nonsense? Do you hear?
Does anybody listen? Can the stones
Bear to listen to this? Do you call it
Nonsense that I poured the waters of my soul
To wash your feet?

SIDI: You did what!

LAKUNLE: Wasted! Wasted! Sidi, my heart
Bursts into flowers with my love.
But you, you and the dead of this village
Trample it with feet of ignorance.

SIDI: [*shakes her head in bafflement.*]
If the snail finds splinters in his shell
He changes house. Why do you stay?

LAKUNLE: Faith. Because I have faith.
Oh Sidi, vow to me your own undying love
And I will scorn the jibes of these bush minds
Who know no better. Swear, Sidi,
Swear you will be my wife and I will
Stand against earth, heaven, and the nine
Hells . . .

SIDI: Now there you go again.
One little thing

And you must chirrup like a cockatoo.
You talk and talk and deafen me
With words which always sound the same
And make no meaning.
I've told you, and I say it again
I shall marry you today, next week
Or any day you name.
But my bride-price must first be paid.
Aha, now you turn away.
But I tell you, Lakunle, I must have
The full bride-price. Will you make me
A laughing-stock? Well, do as you please.
But Sidi will not make herself
A cheap bowl for the village spit.

LAKUNLE: On my head let fall their scorn.

SIDI: They will say I was no virgin
That I was forced to sell my shame
And marry you without a price.

LAKUNLE: A savage custom, barbaric, out-dated,
Rejected, denounced, accursed,
Excommunicated, archaic, degrading,
Humiliating, unspeakable, redundant.
Retrogressive, remarkable, unpalatable.

SIDI: Is the bag empty? Why did you stop?

LAKUNLE: I own only the Shorter Companion
Dictionary, but I have ordered
The Longer One—you wait!

SIDI: Just pay the price.

LAKUNLE: [*with a sudden shout.*]
An ignoble custom, infamous, ignominious
Shaming our heritage before the world.
Sidi, I do not seek a wife
To fetch and carry,
To cook and scrub,

To bring forth children by the gross . . .
SIDI: Heaven forgive you! Do you now scorn
Child-bearing in a wife?
LAKUNLE: Of course I do not. I only mean . . .
Oh Sidi, I want to wed
Because I love,
I seek a life-companion . . .
[*pulpit-declamatory.*]
'And the man shall take the woman
And the two shall be together
As one flesh.'
Sidi, I seek a friend in need.
An equal partner in my race of life.
SIDI: [*attentive no more. Deeply engrossed in counting the beads on her neck.*]
Then pay the price.
LAKUNLE: Ignorant girl, can you not understand?
To pay the price would be
To buy a heifer off the market stall.
You'd be my chattel, my mere property.
No, Sidi! [*very tenderly.*]
When we are wed, you shall not walk or sit
Tethered, as it were, to my dirtied heels.
Together we shall sit at table
—Not on the floor—and eat,
Not with fingers, but with knives
And forks, and breakable plates
Like civilized beings.
I will not have you wait on me
Till I have dined my fill.
No wife of mine, no lawful wedded wife
Shall eat the leavings off my plate—
That is for the children.
I want to walk beside you in the street,

Side by side and arm in arm
Just like the Lagos couples I have seen
High-heeled shoes for the lady, red paint
On her lips. And her hair is stretched
Like a magazine photo. I will teach you
The waltz and we'll both learn the foxtrot
And we'll spend the week-end in night-clubs at Ibadan.
Oh I must show you the grandeur of towns
We'll live there if you like or merely pay visits.
So choose. Be a modern wife, look me in the eye
And give me a little kiss—like this.
[*Kisses her.*]

SIDI: [*backs away.*]
No, don't! I tell you I dislike
This strange unhealthy mouthing you perform.
Every time, your action deceives me
Making me think that you merely wish
To whisper something in my ear.
Then comes this licking of my lips with yours.
It's so unclean. And then,
The sound you make—'Pyout!'
Are you being rude to me?

LAKUNLE: [*wearily.*] It's never any use.
Bush-girl you are, bush-girl you'll always be;
Uncivilized and primitive—bush-girl!
I kissed you as all educated men—
And Christians—kiss their wives.
It is the way of civilized romance.

SIDI: [*lightly.*] A way you mean, to avoid
Payment of lawful bride-price
A cheating way, mean and miserly.

LAKUNLE: [*violently.*] It is not.
[*Sidi bursts out laughing. Lakunle changes his tone to a soulful one, both eyes dreamily shut.*]

Romance is the sweetening of the soul
With fragrance offered by the stricken heart.

SIDI: [*looks at him in wonder for a while.*]
Away with you. The village says you're mad,
And I begin to understand.
I wonder that they let you run the school.
You and your talk. You'll ruin your pupils too
And then they'll utter madness just like you.
[*Noise off-stage.*]
There are people coming
Give me the bucket or they'll jeer.
[*Enter a crowd of youths and drummers, the girls being in various stages of excitement.*]

FIRST GIRL: Sidi, he has returned. He came back just as he said he would.

SIDI: Who has?

FIRST GIRL: The stranger. The man from the outside world.
The clown who fell in the river for you.
[*They all burst out laughing.*]

SIDI: The one who rode on the devil's own horse?

SECOND GIRL: Yes, the same. The stranger with the one-eyed box.
[*She demonstrates the action of a camera amidst admiring titters.*]

THIRD GIRL: And he brought his new horse right into the village square this time. This one has only two feet. You should have seen him. B-r-r-r-r.
[*Runs around the platform driving an imaginary motor-bike.*]

SIDI: And has he brought . . . ?

FIRST GIRL: The images? He brought them all. There was hardly any part of the village which does not show in the book.
[*Clicks the imaginary shutter.*]

SIDI: The book? Did you see the book?
Had he the precious book
That would bestow upon me
Beauty beyond the dreams of a goddess?

For so he said.
The book which would announce
This beauty to the world—
Have you seen it?

THIRD GIRL: Yes, yes, he did. But the Bale is still feasting his eyes on the images. Oh, Sidi, he was right You *are* beautiful. On the cover of the book is an image of you from here [*touches the top of her head*] to here [*her stomach*]. And in the middle leaves, from the beginning of one leaf right across to the end of another, is one of you from head to toe. Do you remember it? It was the one for which he made you stretch your arms towards the sun. [*Rapturously.*] Oh, Sidi, you looked as if, at that moment, the sun himself had been your lover. [*They all gasp with pretended shock at this blasphemy and one slaps her playfully on the buttocks.*]

FIRST GIRL: The Bale is jealous, but he pretends to be proud of you. And when this man tells him how famous you are in the capital, he pretends to be pleased, saying how much honour and fame you have brought to the village.

SIDI: [*with amazement.*] Is not Baroka's image in the book at all?

SECOND GIRL: [*contemptuous.*] Oh yes, it is. But it would have been much better for the Bale if the stranger had omitted him altogether. His image is in a little corner somewhere in the book, and even that corner he shares with one of the village latrines.

SIDI: Is that the truth? Swear! Ask Ogun to
Strike you dead.

GIRL: Ogun strike me dead if I lie.

SIDI: If that is true, then I am more esteemed
Than Bale Baroka,
The Lion of Ilujinle.
This means that I am greater than
The Fox of the Undergrowth,
The living god among men . . .

LAKUNLE: [*peevishly.*] And devil among women.
SIDI: Be silent, you.
    You are merely filled with spite.
LAKUNLE: I know him what he is. This is
    Divine justice that a mere woman
    Should outstrip him in the end.
SIDI: Be quiet;
    Or I swear I'll never speak to you again.
    [*Affects sudden coyness.*]
    In fact, I am not so sure I'll want to wed you now.
LAKUNLE: Sidi!
SIDI: Well, why should I?
    Known as I am to the whole wide world,
    I would demean my worth to wed
    A mere village school teacher.
LAKUNLE: [*in agony.*] Sidi!
SIDI: And one who is too mean
    To pay the bride-price like a man.
LAKUNLE: Oh, Sidi, don't!
SIDI: [*plunging into an enjoyment of Lakunle's misery.*]
    Well, don't you know?
    Sidi is more important even than the Bale.
    More famous than that panther of the trees.
    He is beneath me now—
    Your fearless rake, the scourge of womanhood!
    But now,
    He shares the corner of the leaf
    With the lowest of the low—
    With the dug-out village latrine!
    While I—How many leaves did my own image take?
FIRST GIRL: Two in the middle and . . .
SIDI: No, no. Let the school teacher count!
    How many were there, teacher-man?
LAKUNLE: Three leaves.

SIDI: [*threateningly.*] One leaf for every heart that I shall break.
Beware!
[*Leaps suddenly into the air.*]
Hurray! I'm beautiful!
Hurray for the wandering stranger!

CROWD: Hurray for the Lagos man!

SIDI: [*wildly excited.*] I know. Let us dance the dance of the lost Traveller.

SHOUTS: Yes, let's.

SIDI: Who will dance the devil-horse?
You, you, you and you.
[*The four girls fall out.*]
A python. Who will dance the snake?
Ha ha! Your eyes are shifty and your ways are sly.
[*The selected youth is pushed out amidst jeers.*]
The stranger. We've got to have the being
From the mad outer world . . . You there,
No, you have never felt the surge
Of burning liquor in your milky veins.
Who can we pick that knows the walk of drunks?
You? . . . No, the thought itself
Would knock you out as sure as wine . . . Ah!
[*Turns round slowly to where Lakunle is standing with a kindly, fatherly smile for the children at play.*]
Come on book-worm, you'll play his part.

LAKUNLE: No, no. I've never been drunk in all my life.

SIDI: We know. But your father drank so much,
He must have drunk your share, and that
Of his great grandsons.

LAKUNLE: [*tries to escape.*] I won't take part.

SIDI: You must.

LAKUNLE: I cannot stay. It's nearly time to take
Primary four in Geography.

SIDI: [*goes over to the window and throws it open.*]

Did you think your pupils would remain in school
Now that the stranger has returned?
The village is on holiday, you fool.

LAKUNLE: [*as they drag him towards the platform.*]
No, no. I won't. This foolery bores me.
It is a game of idiots. I have work of more importance.

SIDI: [*bending down over Lakunle who has been seated forcibly on the platform.*]
You are dressed like him
You look like him
You speak his tongue
You think like him
You're just as clumsy
In your Lagos ways—
You'll do for him!

[*This chant is taken up by all and they begin to dance round Lakunle, speaking the words in a fast rhythm. The drummers join in after the first time, keeping up a steady beat as the others whirl round their victim. They go faster and faster and chant faster and faster with each round. By the sixth or seventh, Lakunle has obviously had enough.*]

LAKUNLE: [*raising his voice above the din.*] All right! I'll do it.
Come now, let's get it over with.

[*A terrific shout and a clap of drums. Lakunle enters into the spirit of the dance with enthusiasm. He takes over from Sidi, stations his cast all over the stage as the jungle, leaves the right top-stage clear for the four girls who are to dance the motor-car. A mime follows of the visitor's entry into Ilujinle, and his short stay among the villagers. The four girls crouch on the floor, as four wheels of a car. Lakunle directs their spacing, then takes his place in the middle, and sits on air. He alone does not dance. He does realistic miming. Soft throbbing drums, gradually swelling in volume, and the four 'wheels' begin to rotate the upper halves of their bodies in perpendicular circles. Lakunle clowning the driving motions, obviously enjoying this fully. The drums gain tempo, faster, faster, faster. A sudden*

crash of drums and the girls quiver and dance the stall. Another effort at rhythm fails, and the 'stalling wheels' give a corresponding shudder, finally, and let their faces fall on to their laps. Lakunle tampers with a number of controls, climbs out of the car and looks underneath it. His lips indicate that he is swearing violently. Examines the wheels, pressing them to test the pressure, betrays the devil in him by seizing his chance to pinch the girls' bottoms. One yells and bites him on the ankle. He climbs hurriedly back into the car, makes a final attempt to re-start it, gives it up and decides to abandon it. Picks up his camera and his helmet, pockets a flask of whisky from which he takes a swig, before beginning the trek.
The drums resume beating, a different, darker tone and rhythm, varying with the journey. Full use of 'gangan' and 'iya ilu'. The 'trees' perform a subdued and unobtrusive dance on the same spot. Details as a snake slithering out of the branches and poising over Lakunle's head when he leans against a tree for a rest. He flees, restoring his nerves shortly after by a swig. A monkey drops suddenly in his path and gibbers at him before scampering off. A roar comes from somewhere, etc. His nerves go rapidly and he recuperates himself by copious draughts. He is soon tipsy, battles violently with the undergrowth and curses silently as he swats the flies off his tortured body.
Suddenly, from somewhere in the bush comes the sound of a girl singing. The Traveller shakes his head but the sound persists. Convinced he is suffering from sun-stroke, he drinks again. His last drop, so he tosses the bottle in the direction of the sound, only to be rewarded by a splash, a scream and a torrent of abuse, and finally, silence again. He tip-toes, clears away the obstructing growth, blinks hard and rubs his eyes. Whatever he has seen still remains. He whistles softly, unhitches his camera and begins to jockey himself into a good position for a take. Backwards and forwards, and his eyes are so closely glued to the lens that he puts forward a careless foot and disappears completely. There is a loud splash and the invisible singer alters her next tone to a sustained scream. Quickened

rhythm and shortly afterwards, amidst sounds of splashes, Sidi appears on the stage, with a piece of cloth only partially covering her. Lakunle follows a little later, more slowly, trying to wring out the water from his clothes. He has lost all his appendages except the camera. Sidi has run right across the stage, and returns a short while later, accompanied by the Villagers. The same cast has disappeared and re-forms behind Sidi as the Villagers. They are in an ugly mood, and in spite of his protests, haul him off to the town centre, in front of the 'Odan' tree.

Everything comes to a sudden stop as Baroka the Bale, wiry, goateed, tougher than his sixty-two years, himself emerges at this point from behind the tree. All go down, prostrate or kneeling with the greetings of 'Kabiyesi' 'Baba' etc. All except Lakunle who begins to sneak off.]

BAROKA: Akowe. Teacher wa. Misita Lakunle.

[*As the others take up the cry 'Misita Lakunle' he is forced to stop. He returns and bows deeply from the waist.*]

LAKUNLE: A good morning to you sir.

BAROKA: Guru morin guru morin, ngh-hn! That is
All we get from 'alakowe'. You call at his house
Hoping he sends for beer, but all you get is
Guru morin. Will guru morin wet my throat?
Well, well our man of knowledge, I hope you have no
Query for an old man today.

LAKUNLE: No complaints.

BAROKA: And we are not feuding in something
I have forgotten.

LAKUNLE: Feuding sir? I see no cause at all.

BAROKA: Well, the play was much alive until I came.
And now everything stops, and you were leaving
Us. After all, I knew the story and I came in
Right on cue. It makes me feel as if I was
Chief Baseje.

LAKUNLE: One hardly thinks the Bale would have the time

For such childish nonsense.

BAROKA: A-ah Mister Lakunle. Without these things you call
Nonsense, a Bale's life would be pretty dull.
Well, now that you say I am welcome, shall we
Resume your play?
[*Turns suddenly to his attendants.*]
Seize him!

LAKUNLE: [*momentarily baffled.*] What for? What have I done?

BAROKA: You tried to steal our village maidenhead
Have you forgotten? If he has, serve him a slap
To wake his brain.

[*An uplifted arm being proffered, Lakunle quickly recollects and nods his head vigorously. So the play is back in performance. The Villagers gather round threatening, clamouring for his blood. Lakunle tries bluff, indignation, appeasement in turn. At a sudden signal from the Bale, they throw him down prostrate on his face. Only then does the Chief begin to show him sympathy, appear to understand the Stranger's plight, and pacify the villagers on his behalf. He orders dry clothes for him, seats him on his right and orders a feast in his honour. The Stranger springs up every second to take photographs of the party, but most of the time his attention is fixed on Sidi dancing with abandon. Eventually he whispers to the Chief, who nods in consent, and Sidi is sent for. The Stranger arranges Sidi in all sorts of magazine postures and takes innumerable photographs of her. Drinks are pressed upon him; he refuses at first, eventually tries the local brew with scepticism, appears to relish it, and drinks profusely. Before long, however, he leaves the party to be sick. They clap him on the back as he goes out, and two drummers who insist on dancing round him nearly cause the calamity to happen on the spot. However, he rushes out with his hand held to the mouth. Lakunle's exit seems to signify the end of the mime. He returns almost at once and the others discard their roles.*]

SIDI: [*delightedly.*] What did I say? You played him to the bone,
A court jester would have been the life for you,

Instead of school.
[*Points contemptuously to the school.*]

BAROKA: And where would the village be, robbed of
Such wisdom as Mister Lakunle dispenses
Daily? Who would tell us where we go wrong?
Eh, Mister Lakunle?

SIDI: [*hardly listening, still in the full grip of her excitement.*]
Who comes with me to find the man?
But Lakunle, you'll have to come and find sense
In his clipping tongue. You see book-man
We cannot really do
Without your head.
[*Lakunle begins to protest, but they crowd him and try to bear him down. Suddenly he breaks free and takes to his heels with all the women in full pursuit. Baroka is left sitting by himself—his wrestler, who accompanied him on his entry, stands a respectful distance away—staring at the flock of women in flight. From the folds of his agbada he brings out his copy of the magazine and admires the heroine of the publication. Nods slowly to himself.*]

BAROKA: Yes, yes . . . it is five full months since last
I took a wife . . . five full months . . .

NOON

A road by the market. Enter Sidi, happily engrossed in the pictures of herself in the magazine. Lakunle follows one or two paces behind carrying a bundle of firewood which Sidi has set out to obtain. They are met in the centre by Sadiku, who has entered from the opposite side. Sadiku is an old woman, with a shawl over her head.

SADIKU: Fortune is with me. I was going to your house to see you.
SIDI: [*startled out of her occupation.*] What! Oh, it is you, Sadiku.
SADIKU: The Lion sent me. He wishes you well.
SIDI: Thank him for me.
[*Then excitedly.*]
Have you seen these?
Have you seen these images of me
Wrought by the man from the capital city?
Have you felt the gloss? [*Caresses the page.*]
Smoother by far than the parrot's breast.
SADIKU: I have. I have. I saw them as soon as the city man came . . . Sidi, I bring a message from my lord. [*Jerks her head at Lakunle.*] Shall we draw aside a little?
SIDI: Him? Pay no more heed to that
Than you would a eunuch.
SADIKU: Then, in as few words as it takes to tell, Baroka wants you for a wife.
LAKUNLE: [*bounds forward, dropping the wood.*]
What! The greedy dog!
Insatiate camel of a foolish, doting race;
Is he at his tricks again?
SIDI: Be quiet, 'Kunle. You get so tiresome.
The message is for me, not you.
LAKUNLE: [*down on his knees at once. Covers Sidi's hands with kisses.*]

My Ruth, my Rachel, Esther, Bathsheba
Thou sum of fabled perfections
From Genesis to the Revelations
Listen not to the voice of this infidel . . .

SIDI: [*snatches her hand away.*]
Now that's your other game;
Giving me funny names you pick up
In your wretched books.
My name is Sidi. And now, let me be.
My name is Sidi, and I am beautiful.
The stranger took my beauty
And placed it in my hands.
Here, here it is. I need no funny names
To tell me of my fame.
Loveliness beyond the jewels of a throne—
That is what he said.

SADIKU: [*gleefully.*] Well, will you be Baroka's own jewel? Will you be his sweetest princess, soothing him on weary nights? What answer shall I give my lord?

SIDI: [*wags her finger playfully at the woman.*]
Ha ha. Sadiku of the honey tongue.
Sadiku, head of the Lion's wives.
You'll make no prey of Sidi with your wooing tongue
Not this Sidi whose fame has spread to Lagos
And beyond the seas.
[*Lakunle beams with satisfaction and rises.*]

SADIKU: Sidi, have you considered what a life of bliss awaits you? Baroka swears to take no other wife after you. Do you know what it is to be the Bale's last wife? I'll tell you. When he dies—and that should not be long; even the Lion has to die sometime—well, when he does, it means that you will have the honour of being the senior wife of the new Bale. And just think, until Baroka dies, you shall be his favourite. No living in the outhouses for you, my girl. Your place will always be in the palace; first as the latest bride, and afterwards, as the head of the new harem . . . It is a rich life, Sidi. I know. I have been in that position for forty-one years.

SIDI: You waste your breath.
Why did Baroka not request my hand
Before the stranger
Brought his book of images?
Why did the Lion not bestow his gift
Before my face was lauded to the world?
Can you not see? Because he sees my worth
Increased and multiplied above his own;
Because he can already hear
The ballad-makers and their songs
In praise of Sidi, the incomparable,
While the Lion is forgotten.
He seeks to have me as his property
Where I must fade beneath his jealous hold.
Ah, Sadiku,
The school-man here has taught me certain things
And my images have taught me all the rest.
Baroka merely seeks to raise his manhood
Above my beauty
He seeks new fame
As the one man who has possessed
The jewel of Ilujinle!

SADIKU: [*shocked, bewildered, incapable of making any sense of Sidi's words.*] But Sidi, are you well? Such nonsense never passed your lips before. Did you not sound strange, even in your own hearing? [*Rushes suddenly at Lakunle.*] Is this your doing, you popinjay? Have you driven the poor girl mad at last? Such rubbish . . . I will beat your head for this!

LAKUNLE: [*retreating in panic.*] Keep away from me, old hag.

SIDI: Sadiku, let him be.

Tell your lord that I can read his mind,
That I will none of him.
Look—judge for yourself.
[*Opens the magazine and points out the pictures.*]
He's old. I never knew till now,
He was that old . . .
[*During the rest of her speech, Sidi runs her hand over the surface of the relevant part of the photographs, tracing the contours with her fingers.*]
. . . To think I took
No notice of my velvet skin.
How smooth it is!
And no man ever thought
To praise the fulness of my breasts . . .

LAKUNLE: [*laden with guilt and full of apology.*]
Well, Sidi, I did think . . .
But somehow it was not the proper thing.

SIDI: [*ignores the interruption.*]
See I hold them to the warm caress
[*unconsciously pushes out her chest.*]
Of a desire-filled sun.
[*Smiles mischievously.*]
There's a deceitful message in my eyes
Beckoning insatiate men to certain doom.
And teeth that flash the sign of happiness,
Strong and evenly, beaming full of life.
Be just, Sadiku,
Compare my image and your lord's—
An age of difference!
See how the water glistens on my face
Like the dew-moistened leaves on a Harmattan morning
But he—his face is like a leather piece
Torn rudely from the saddle of his horse,
[*Sadiku gasps.*]

Sprinkled with the musty ashes
From a pipe that is long over-smoked.
And this goat-like tuft
Which I once thought was manly;
It is like scattered twists of grass—
Not even green—
But charred and lifeless, as after a forest fire!
Sadiku, I am young and brimming; he is spent.
I am the twinkle of a jewel
But he is the hind-quarters of a lion!

SADIKU: [*recovering at last from helpless amazement.*] May Sango restore your wits. For most surely some angry god has taken possession of you. [*Turns around and walks away. Stops again as she remembers something else.*] Your ranting put this clean out of my head. My lord says that if you would not be his wife, would you at least come to supper at his house tonight. There is a small feast in your honour. He wishes to tell you how happy he is that the great capital city has done so much honour to a daughter of Ilujinle. You have brought great fame to your people.

SIDI: Ho ho! Do you think that I was only born
Yesterday?
The tales of Baroka's little suppers,
I know all.
Tell your lord that Sidi does not sup with
Married men.

SADIKU: They are lies, lies. You must not believe everything you hear. Sidi, would I deceive you? I swear to you . . .

SIDI: Can you deny that
Every woman who has supped with him one night,
Becomes his wife or concubine the next.

LAKUNLE: Is it for nothing he is called the Fox?

SADIKU: [*advancing on him.*] You keep out of this, or so Sango be my witness . . .

LAKUNLE: [*retreats just a little, but continues to talk.*]
His wiliness is known even in the larger towns.
Did you never hear
Of how he foiled the Public Works attempt
To build the railway through Ilujinle.
SADIKU: Nobody knows the truth of that. It is all hearsay.
SIDI: I love hearsays. Lakunle, tell me all.
LAKUNLE: Did you not know it? Well sit down and listen.
My father told me, before he died. And few men
Know of this trick—oh he's a die-hard rogue
Sworn against our progress . . . yes . . . it was . . . somewhere here
The track should have been laid just along
The outskirts. Well, the workers came, in fact
It was prisoners who were brought to do
The harder part . . . to break the jungle's back . . .
[*Enter the prisoners, guarded by two warders. A white surveyor examines his map (khaki helmet, spats, etc.) The foreman runs up with his camp stool, table etc., erects the umbrella over him and unpacks the usual box of bush comforts—soda siphon, whisky bottle and geometric sandwiches. His map consulted, he directs the sweat team where to work. They begin felling, matchet swinging, log dragging, all to the rhythm of the work gang's metal percussion (rod on gong or rude triangle, etc.) The two performers are also the song leaders and the others fill the chorus. 'N'ijo itoro', 'Amuda el 'ebe l'aiya' 'Gbe je on'ipa' etc.*]
LAKUNLE: They marked the route with stakes, ate
Through the jungle and began the tracks. Trade,
Progress, adventure, success, civilization,
Fame, international conspicuousity . . . it was
All within the grasp of Ilujinle . . .
[*The wrestler enters, stands horrified at the sight and flees. Returns later with the Bale himself who soon assesses the situation. They disappear. The work continues, the surveyor occupies himself*

with the fly-whisk and whisky. Shortly after, a bull-roarer is heard. The prisoners falter a little, pick up again. The bull-roarer continues on its way, nearer and farther, moving in circles, so that it appears to come from all round them. The foreman is the first to break and then the rest is chaos. Sole survivor of the rout is the surveyor who is too surprised to move.

Baroka enters a few minutes later accompanied by some attendants and preceded by a young girl bearing a calabash bowl. The surveyor, angry and threatening, is prevailed upon to open his gift. From it he reveals a wad of pound notes and kola nuts. Mutual understanding is established. The surveyor frowns heavily, rubs his chin and consults his map. Re-examines the contents of the bowl, shakes his head. Baroka adds more money, and a coop of hens. A goat follows, and more money. This time 'truth' dawns on him at last, he has made a mistake. The track really should go the other way. What an unfortunate error, discovered just in time! No, no, no possibility of a mistake this time, the track should be much further away. In fact (scooping up the soil) the earth is most unsuitable, couldn't possibly support the weight of a railway engine. A gourd of palm wine is brought to seal the agreement and a kola nut is broken. Baroka's men help the surveyor pack and they leave with their arms round each other followed by the surveyor's booty.]

LAKUNLE: [*as the last of the procession disappears, shakes his fist at them, stamping on the ground.*]

Voluptuous beast! He loves this life too well
To bear to part from it. And motor roads
And railways would do just that, forcing
Civilization at his door. He foresaw it
And he barred the gates, securing fast
His dogs and horses, his wives and all his
Concubines . . . ah, yes . . . all those concubines
Baroka has such a selective eye, none suits him
But the best . . .

[*His eyes truly light up. Sidi and Sadiku snigger, tip-toe off stage.*]
. . . Yes, one must grant him that.
Ah, I sometimes wish I led his kind of life.
Such luscious bosoms make his nightly pillow.
I am sure he keeps a time-table just as
I do at school. Only way to ensure fair play.
He must be healthy to keep going as he does.
I don't know what the women see in him. His eyes
Are small and always red with wine. He must
Possess some secret . . . No! I do not envy him!
Just the one woman for me. Alone I stand
For progress, with Sidi my chosen soul-mate, the one
Woman of my life . . . Sidi! Sidi where are you?
[*Rushes out after them, returns to fetch the discarded firewood and runs out again.*]

*

[*Baroka in bed, naked except for baggy trousers, calf-length. It is a rich bedroom covered in animal skins and rugs. Weapons round the wall. Also a strange machine, a most peculiar contraption with a long lever. Kneeling beside the bed is Baroka's current Favourite, engaged in plucking the hairs from his armpit. She does this by first massaging the spot around the selected hair very gently with her forefinger. Then, with hardly a break, she pulls out the hair between her finger and the thumb with a sudden sharp movement. Baroka twitches slightly with each pull. Then an aspirated 'A-ah', and a look of complete beatitude spreads all over his face.*]

FAVOURITE: Do I improve my lord?

BAROKA: You are still somewhat over-gentle with the pull
As if you feared to hurt the panther of the trees.
Be sharp and sweet
Like the swift sting of a vicious wasp
For there the pleasure lies—the cooling aftermath.

FAVOURITE: I'll learn, my lord.

BAROKA: You have not time, my dear.
Tonight I hope to take another wife.
And the honour of this task, you know,
Belongs by right to my latest choice.
But—A-ah—Now that was sharp.
It had in it the scorpion's sudden sting
Without its poison.
It was an angry pull; you tried to hurt
For I had made you wrathful with my boast.
But now your anger flows in my blood-stream.
How sweet it is! A-ah! That was sweeter still.
I think perhaps that I shall let you stay,
The sole out-puller of my sweat-bathed hairs.
Ach!
[*Sits up suddenly and rubs the sore point angrily.*]
Now that had far more pain than pleasure
Venegeful creature, you did not caress
The area of extraction long enough!
[*Enter Sadiku. She goes down on her knees at once and bows her head into her lap.*]
Aha! Here comes Sadiku.
Do you bring some balm,
To soothe the smart of my misused armpit?
Away, you enemy!
[*Exit the Favourite.*]

SADIKU: My lord . . .

BAROKA: You have my leave to speak.
What did she say?

SADIKU: She will not, my lord. I did my best, but she will have none of you.

BAROKA: It follows the pattern—a firm refusal
At the start. Why will she not?

SADIKU: That is the strange part of it. She say's you're much too old. If you ask me, I think that she is really off her head. All this excitement of the books has been too much for her.

BAROKA: [*springs to his feet.*]
She says . . . That I am old
That I am much too old? Did a slight
Unripened girl say this of me?

SADIKU: My lord, I heard the incredible words with my ears, and I thought the world was mad.

BAROKA: But is it possible, Sadiku? Is this right?
Did I not, at the festival of Rain,
Defeat the men in the log-tossing match?
Do I not still with the most fearless ones,
Hunt the leopard and the boa at night
And save the farmers' goats from further harm?
And does she say I'm old?
Did I not, to announce the Harmattan,
Climb to the top of the silk-cotton tree,
Break the first pod, and scatter tasselled seeds
To the four winds—and this but yesterday?
Do any of my wives report
A failing in my manliness?
The strongest of them all
Still wearies long before the Lion does!
And so would she, had I the briefest chance
To teach this unfledged birdling
That lacks the wisdom to embrace
The rich mustiness of age . . . if I could once . . .
Come hither, soothe me, Sadiku
For I am wroth at heart.
[*Lies back on the bed, staring up as before. Sadiku takes her place at the foot of the bed and begins to tickle the soles of his feet. Baroka turns to the left suddenly, reaches down the side, and comes up with a copy of the magazine. Opens it and begins to study the pictures. He heaves a long sigh.*]

That is good, Sadiku, very good.
[*He begins to compare some pictures in the book, obviously his own and Sidi's. Flings the book away suddenly and stares at the ceiling for a second or two. Then, unsmiling.*]
Perhaps it is as well, Sadiku.

SADIKU: My lord, what did you say?

BAROKA: Yes, faithful one, I say it is as well.
The scorn, the laughter and the jeers
Would have been bitter.
Had she consented and my purpose failed,
I would have sunk with shame.

SADIKU: My lord, I do not understand.

BAROKA: The time has come when I can fool myself
No more. I am no man, Sadiku. My manhood
Ended near a week ago.

SADIKU: The gods forbid.

BAROKA: I wanted Sidi because I still hoped—
A foolish thought I know, but still—I hoped
That, with a virgin young and hot within,
My failing strength would rise and save my pride.
[*Sadiku begins to moan.*]
A waste of hope. I knew it even then.
But it's a human failing never to accept
The worst; and so I pandered to my vanity.
When manhood must, it ends.
The well of living, tapped beyond its depth,
Dries up, and mocks the wastrel in the end.
I am withered and unsapped, the joy
Of ballad-mongers, the aged butt
Of youth's ribaldry.

SADIKU: [*tearfully.*] The Gods must have mercy yet.

BAROKA: [*as if suddenly aware of her presence, starts up.*]
I have told this to no one but you,
Who are my eldest, my most faithful wife.

But if you dare parade my shame before the world . . .
[*Sadiku shakes her head in protest and begins to stroke the soles of his feet with renewed tenderness. Baroka sighs and falls back slowly.*]
How irritable I have grown of late
Such doubts to harbour of your loyalty . . .
But this disaster is too much for one
Checked thus as I upon the prime of youth.
That rains that blessed me from my birth
Number a meagre sixty-two;
While my grandfather, that man of teak,
Fathered two sons, late on sixty-five.
But Okiki, my father beat them all
Producing female twins at sixty-seven.
Why then must I, descendant of these lions
Forswear my wives at a youthful sixty-two
My veins of life run dry, my manhood gone!
[*His voice goes drowsy; Sadiku sighs and moans and caresses his feet. His face lights up suddenly with rapture.*]
Sango bear witness! These weary feet
Have felt the loving hands of much design
In women.
My soles have felt the scratch of harsh,
Gravelled hands.
They have borne the heaviness of clumsy,
Gorilla paws.
And I have known the tease of tiny,
Dainty hands,
Toy-like hands that tantalized
My eager senses,
Promised of thrills to come
Remaining
Unfulfilled because the fingers
Were too frail

The touch too light and faint to pierce
The incredible thickness of my soles.
But thou Sadiku, thy plain unadorned hands
Encase a sweet sensuality which age
Will not destroy. A-ah,
Oyayi! Beyond a doubt Sadiku,
Thou art the queen of them all.
[*Falls asleep.*]

NIGHT

The village centre. Sidi stands by the Schoolroom window, admiring her photos as before. Enter Sadiku with a longish bundle. She is very furtive. Unveils the object which turns out to be a carved figure of the Bale, naked and in full detail. She takes a good look at it, bursts suddenly into derisive laughter, sets the figure standing in front of the tree. Sidi stares in utter amazement.

SADIKU: So we did for you too did we? We did for you in the end. Oh high and mighty lion, have we really scotched you? A—ya-ya-ya . . . we women undid you in the end. I was there when it happened to your father, the great Okiki. I did for him, I, the youngest and freshest of the wives. I killed him with my strength. I called him and he came at me, but no, for him, this was not like other times. I, Sadiku, was I not flame itself and he the flax on old women's spindles? I ate him up! Race of mighty lions, we always consume you, at our pleasure we spin you, at our whim we make you dance; like the foolish top you think the world revolves around you . . . fools! fools! . . . it is you who run giddy while we stand still and watch, and draw your frail thread from you, slowly, till nothing is left but a runty old stick. I scotched Okiki, Sadiku's unopened treasure-house demanded sacrifice, and Okiki came with his rusted key. Like a snake he came at me, like a rag he went back, a limp rag, smeared in shame. . . . [*Her ghoulish laugh re-possesses her.*] Ah, take warning my masters, we'll scotch you in the end . . . [*With a yell she leaps up, begins to dance round the tree, chanting.*]
Take warning, my masters
We'll scotch you in the end.

[*Sidi shuts the window gently, comes out, Sadiku, as she comes round again, gasps and is checked in mid-song.*]

SADIKU: Oh it is you my daughter. You should have chosen a better time to scare me to death. The hour of victory is no time for any woman to die.

SIDI: Why? What battle have you won?

SADIKU: Not me alone girl. You too. Every woman. Oh my daughter, that I have lived to see this day . . . To see him fizzle with the drabbest puff of a mis-primed 'sakabula'.
[*Resumes her dance.*]
Take warning, my masters
We'll scotch you in the end.

SIDI: Wait Sadiku. I cannot understand.

SADIKU: You will my girl. You will.
Take warning my masters . . ,

SIDI: Sadiku, are you well?

SADIKU: Ask no questions my girl. Just join my victory dance. Oh Sango my lord, who of us possessed your lightning and ran like fire through that lion's tail . . .

SIDI: [*holds her firmly as she is about to go off again.*]
Stop your loose ranting. You will not
Move from here until you make some sense.

SADIKU: Oh you are troublesome. Do you promise to tell no one?

SIDI: I swear it. Now tell me quickly.
[*As Sadiku whispers, her eyes widen.*]
O-ho-o-o-o-!
But Sadiku, if he knew the truth, why
Did he ask me to . . .
[*Again Sadiku whispers.*]
Ha ha! Some hope indeed. Oh Sadiku
I suddenly am glad to be a woman.
[*Leaps in the air.*]
We won! We won! Hurray for womankind!
[*Falls in behind Sadiku.*]

Take warning, my masters
We'll scotch you in the end. [*Lakunle enters unobserved.*]

LAKUNLE: The full moon is not yet, but
The women cannot wait.
They must go mad without it.
[*The dancing stops. Sadiku frowns.*]

SADIKU: The scarecrow is here. Begone fop! This is the world of women. At this moment our star sits in the centre of the sky. We are supreme. What is more, we are about to perform a ritual. If you remain, we will chop you up, we will make you the sacrifice.

LAKUNLE: What is the hag gibbering?

SADIKU: [*advances menacingly.*] You less than man, you less than the littlest woman, I say begone!

LAKUNLE: [*nettled.*] I will have you know that I am a man
As you will find out if you dare
To lay a hand on me.

SADIKU: [*throws back her head in laughter.*] You a man? Is Baroka not more of a man than you? And if he is no longer a man, then what are you? [*Lakunle, understanding the meaning, stands rooted, shocked.*] Come on, dear girl, let him look on if he will. After all, only *men* are barred from watching this ceremony.
Take warning, my masters
We'll . . .

SIDI: Stop. Sadiku stop. Oh such an idea
Is running in my head. Let me to the palace for
This supper he promised me. Sadiku, what a way
To mock the devil. I shall ask forgiveness
For my hasty words . . . No need to change
My answer and consent to be his bride—he might
Suspect you've told me. But I shall ask a month
To think on it.

SADIKU: [*somewhat doubtful.*] Baroka is no child you know, he will know I have betrayed him.

SIDI: No, he will not. Oh Sadiku let me go.
I long to see him thwarted, to watch his longing
His twitching hands which this time cannot
Rush to loosen his trouser cords.

SADIKU: You will have to match the Fox's cunning. Use your bashful looks and be truly repentant. Goad him my child, torment him until he weeps for shame.

SIDI: Leave it to me. He will never suspect you
of deceit.

SADIKU: [*with another of her energetic leaps.*] Yo-rooo o! Yo-rororo o!
Shall I come with you?

SIDI: Will that be wise? You forget
We have not seen each other.

SADIKU: Away then. Away woman. I shall bide here.
Haste back and tell Sadiku how the no-man is.
Away, my lovely child.

LAKUNLE: [*he has listened with increasing horror.*]
No, Sidi, don't. If you care
One little bit for what I feel,
Do not go to torment the man.
Suppose he knows that you have come to jeer—
And he will know, if he is not a fool—
He is a savage thing, degenerate
He would beat a helpless woman if he could . . .

SIDI: [*running off gleefully.*] Ta-raa school teacher. Wait here for me.

LAKUNLE: [*stamps his foot helplessly.*]
Foolish girl! . . . And this is all your work.
Could you not keep a secret?
Must every word leak out of you
As surely as the final drops
Of mother's milk
Oozed from your flattened breast
Generations ago?

SADIKU: Watch your wagging tongue, unformed creature!

LAKUNLE: If any harm befalls her . . .

SADIKU: Woman though she is, she can take better care of herself than you can of her. Fancy a thing like you actually wanting a girl like that, all to your little self. [*Walks round him and looks him up and down.*] Ah! Oba Ala is an accommodating god. What a poor figure you cut!

LAKUNLE: I wouldn't demean myself to bandy words
With a woman of the bush.

SADIKU: At this moment, your betrothed is supping
with the Lion.

LAKUNLE: [*pleased at the use of the word 'Betrothed'.*]
Well, we are not really betrothed as yet,
I mean, she is not promised yet.
But it will come in time, I'm sure.

SADIKU: [*bursts into her cackling laughter,*] The bride-price, is that paid?

LAKUNLE: Mind your own business.

SADIKU: Why don't you do what other men have done. Take a farm for a season. One harvest will be enough to pay the price, even for a girl like Sidi. Or will the smell of the wet soil be too much for your delicate nostrils?

LAKUNLE: I said mind your own business.

SADIKU: A—a—ah. It is true what they say then. You are going to convert the whole village so that no one will ever pay the bride-price again. Ah, you're a clever man. I must admit that it is a good way for getting out of it, but don't you think you'd use more time and energy that way than you would if . . .

LAKUNLE: [*with conviction.*] Within a year or two, I swear,
This town shall see a transformation
Bride-price will be a thing forgotten
And wives shall take their place by men.
A motor road will pass this spot.

And bring the city ways to us.
We'll buy saucepans for all the women
Clay pots are crude and unhygienic
No man shall take more wives than one
That's why they're impotent too soon.
The ruler shall ride cars, not horses
Or a bicycle at the very least.
We'll burn the forest, cut the trees
Then plant a modern park for lovers
We'll print newspapers every day
With pictures of seductive girls.
The world will judge our progress by
The girls that win beauty contests.
While Lagos builds new factories daily
We only play 'ayo' and gossip.
Where is our school of Ballroom dancing?
Who here can throw a cocktail party?
We must be modern with the rest
Or live forgotten by the world
We must reject the palm wine habit.
And take to tea, with milk and sugar.
[*Turns on Sadiku who has been staring at him in terror. She retreats, and he continues to talk down at her as they go round, then down and off-stage, Lakunle's hectoring voice trailing away in the distance.*]
This is my plan, you withered face
And I shall start by teaching you.
From now you shall attend my school
And take your place with twelve-year olds.
For though you're nearly seventy,
Your mind is simple and unformed.
Have you no shame that at your age,
You neither read nor write nor think?
You spend your days as senior wife,

Collecting brides for Baroka.
And now because you've sucked him dry,
You send my Sidi to his shame. . . .
[*The scene changes to Baroka's bedroom. On the left in a one-knee-on-floor posture, two men are engaged in a kind of wrestling, their arms clasped round each other's waist, testing the right moment to leave. One is Baroka, the other a short squat figure of apparent muscular power. The contest is still in the balanced stage. In some distant part of the house, Sidi's voice is heard lifted in the familiar general greeting, addressed to no one in particular.*]

SIDI: A good day to the head and people
Of this house.
[*Baroka lifts his head, frowns as if he is trying to place the voice.*]
A good day to the head and people
Of this house.
[*Baroka now decides to ignore it and to concentrate on the contest. Sidi's voice draws progressively nearer. She enters nearly backwards, as she is still busy admiring the room through which she has just passed. Gasps on turning round to see the two men.*]

BAROKA: [*without looking up.*] Is Sadiku not at home then?

SIDI: [*absent-mindedly.*] Hm?

BAROKA: I asked, is Sadiku not at home?

SIDI: [*recollecting herself, she curtsys quickly.*] I saw no one, Baroka.

BAROKA: No one? Do you mean there was no one
To bar unwanted strangers from my privacy?

SIDI: [*retreating.*] The house . . . seemed . . . empty.

BAROKA: Ah, I forget. This is the price I pay
Once every week, for being progressive.
Prompted by the school teacher, my servants
Were prevailed upon to form something they call
The Palace Workers' Union. And in keeping
With the habits—I am told—of modern towns,
This is their day off.

SIDI: [*seeing that Baroka seems to be in a better mood, she becomes somewhat bolder. Moves forward—saucily.*]
Is this also a day off
For Baroka's wives?

BAROKA: [*looks up sharply, relaxes and speaks with a casual voice.*]
No, the madness has not gripped them—yet.
Did you not meet with one of them?

SIDI: No, Baroka. There was no one about.

BAROKA: Not even Ailatu, my favourite?
Was she not at her usual place,
Beside my door?

SIDI: [*absently. She is deeply engrossed in watching the contest.*]
Her stool is there. And I saw
The slippers she was embroidering.

BAROKA: Hm. Hm. I think I know
Where she'll be found. In a dark corner
Sulking like a slighted cockroach.
By the way, look and tell me
If she left her shawl behind.
[*So as not to miss any part of the tussle, she moves backwards, darts a quick look round the door and back again.*]

SIDI: There is a black shawl on the stool.

BAROKA: [*a regretful sigh.*]
Then she'll be back tonight. I had hoped
My words were harsh enough
To free me from her spite for a week or more.

SIDI: Did Ailatu offend her husband?

BAROKA: Offend? My armpit still weeps blood
For the gross abuse I suffered from one
I called my favourite.

SIDI: [*in a disappointed voice.*]
Oh. Is that all?

BAROKA: Is that not enough? Why child?
What more could the woman do?

SIDI: Nothing. Nothing, Baroka. I thought perhaps—
Well—young wives are known to be—
Forward—sometimes—to their husbands.

BAROKA: In an ill-kept household perhaps. But not
Under Baroka's roof. And yet,
Such are the sudden spites of women
That even I cannot foresee them all.
And child—if I lose this little match
Remember that my armpit
Burns and itches turn by turn.
[*Sidi continues watching for some time, then clasps her hand over her mouth as she remembers what she should have done to begin with. Doubtful how to proceed, she hesitates for some moments, then comes to a decision and kneels.*]

SIDI: I have come, Bale, as a repentant child.

BAROKA: What?

SIDI: [*very hesitantly, eyes to the floor, but she darts a quick look up when she thinks the Bale isn't looking.*]
The answer which I sent to the Bale
Was given in a thoughtless moment . . .

BAROKA: Answer, child? To what?

SIDI: A message brought by . . .

BAROKA: [*groans and strains in a muscular effort.*]
Will you say that again? It is true that for supper
I did require your company. But up till now
Sadiku has brought no reply.

SIDI: [*amazed.*] But the other matter! Did not the Bale
Send . . . did Baroka not send . . . ?

BAROKA: [*with sinister encouragement.*]
What did Baroka not, my child?

SIDI: [*cowed, but angry, rises.*]
It is nothing, Bale. I only hope
That I am here at the Bale's invitation.

BAROKA: [*as if trying to understand, he frowns as he looks at her.*]

A-ah, at last I understand. You think
I took offence because you entered
Unannounced?

SIDI: I remember that the Bale called me
An unwanted stranger.

BAROKA: That could be expected. Is a man's bedroom
To be made naked to any flea
That chances to wander through?
[*Sidi turns away, very hurt.*]
Come, come, my child. You are too quick
To feel aggrieved. Of course you are
More than welcome. But I expected Ailatu
To tell me you were here.
[*Sidi curtsys briefly with her back to Baroka. After a while, she turns round. The mischief returns to her face. Baroka's attitude of denial has been a set-back but she is now ready to pursue her mission.*]

SIDI: I hope the Bale will not think me
Forward. But, like everyone, I had thought
The Favourite was a gentle woman.

BAROKA: And so had I.

SIDI: [*slyly.*] One would hardly think that *she*
Would give offence without a cause
Was the Favourite . . . in some way . . .
Dissatisfied . . . with her lord and husband?
[*With a mock curtsy, quickly executed as Baroka begins to look up.*]

BAROKA: [*slowly turns towards her.*]
Now that
Is a question which I never thought to hear
Except from a school teacher. Do you think
The Lion has such leisure that he asks
The whys and wherefores of a woman's
Squint?

[*Sidi steps back and curtsys. As before, and throughout this scene, she is easily cowed by Baroka's change of mood, all the more easily as she is, in any case, frightened by her own boldness.*]

SIDI: I meant no disrespect . . .

BAROKA: [*gently.*] I know. [*Breaks off.*] Christians on my
Father's shrines, child!
Do you think I took offence? A—aw
Come in and seat yourself. Since you broke in
Unawares, and appear resolved to stay,
Try, if you can, not to make me feel
A humourless old ram. I allow no one
To watch my daily exercise, but as we say,
The woman gets lost in the woods one day
And every wood deity dies the next.

[*Sidi curtsys, watches and moves forward warily, as if expecting the two men to spring apart too suddenly.*]

SIDI: I think he will win.

BAROKA: Is that a wish, my daughter?

SIDI: No, but—[*Hesitates, but boldness wins.*]
If the tortoise cannot tumble
It does not mean that he can stand.

[*Baroka looks at her, seemingly puzzled. Sidi turns away, humming.*]

BAROKA: When the child is full of riddles, the mother
Has one water-pot the less.

[*Sidi tiptoes to Baroka's back and pulls asses' ears at him.*]

SIDI: I think he will win.

BAROKA: He knows he must. Would it profit me
To pit my strength against a weakling?
Only yesterday, this son of—I suspect—
A python for a mother, and fathered beyond doubt
By a blubber-bottomed baboon,
[*The complimented man grins.*]
Only yesterday, he nearly

Ploughed my tongue with my front teeth
In a friendly wrestling bout.

WRESTLER: [*encouraged, makes an effort.*] Ugh. Ugh.

SIDI: [*bent almost over them. Genuinely worried.*]
Oh! Does it hurt?

BAROKA: Not yet . . . but, as I was saying
I change my wrestlers when I have learnt
To throw them. I also change my wives
When I have learnt to tire them.

SIDI: And is this another . . . changing time
For the Bale?

BAROKA: Who knows? Until the finger nails
Have scraped the dust, no one can tell
Which insect released his bowels.
[*Sidi grimaces in disgust and walks away. Returns as she thinks up a new idea.*]

SIDI: A woman spoke to me this afternoon.

BAROKA: Indeed. And does Sidi find this unusual—
That a woman speak with her in the afternoon?

SIDI: [*stamping.*] No. She had the message of a go-between.

BAROKA: Did she? Then I rejoice with you.
[*Sidi stands biting her lips. Baroka looks at her, this time with deliberate appreciation.*]
And now I think of it, why not?
There must be many men who
Build their loft to fit your height.

SIDI: [*unmoving, pointedly.*] Her message came from one
With many lofts.

BAROKA: Ah! Such is the greed of men.

SIDI: If Baroka were my father
[*aside*]—which many would take him to be—
[*Makes a rude sign.*]
Would he pay my dowry to this man
And give his blessings?

BAROKA: Well, I must know his character.
For instance, is the man rich?
SIDI: Rumour has it so.
BAROKA: Is he repulsive?
SIDI: He is old. [*Baroka winces.*]
BAROKA: Is he mean and miserly?
SIDI: To strangers—no. There are tales
Of his open-handedness, which are never
Quite without a motive. But his wives report
—To take one little story—
How he grew the taste for ground corn
And pepper—because he would not pay
The price of snuff!
[*With a sudden burst of angry energy, Baroka lifts his opponent and throws him over his shoulder.*]
BAROKA: A lie! The price of snuff
Had nothing to do with it.
SIDI: [*too excited to listen.*] You won!
BAROKA: By the years on my beard, I swear
They slander me!
SIDI: [*excitedly.*] You won. You won!
[*She breaks into a kind of shoulder dance and sings.*]
Yokolu Yokolu. Ko ha tan bi
Iyawo gb'oko san'le
Oko yo 'ke . . .
[*She repeats this throughout Baroka's protests. Baroka is pacing angrily up and down. The defeated man, nursing a hip, goes to the corner of the room and lifts out a low 'ako' bench. He sits on the floor, and soon, Baroka joins him; using only their arms now, they place their elbows on the bench and grip hands. Baroka takes his off again, replaces it, takes it off again and so on during the rest of his outburst.*]
BAROKA: This means nothing to me of course. Nothing!
But I know the ways of women, and I know

Their ruinous tongues.
Suppose that, as a child—only suppose—
Suppose then, that as a child, I—
And remember, I only use myself
To illustrate the plight of many men . . .
So, once again, suppose that as a child
I grew to love 'tanfiri'—with a good dose of pepper
And growing old, I found that—
Sooner than die away, my passion only
Bred itself upon each mouthful of
Ground corn and pepper I consumed.
Now, think child, would it be seemly
At my age, and the father of children,
To be discovered, in public
Thrusting fistfuls of corn and pepper
In my mouth? Is it not wise to indulge
In the little masquerade of a dignified
Snuff-box?—But remember, I only make
A pleading for this prey of women's
Malice. I feel his own injustice,
Being myself, a daily fellow-sufferer!
[*Baroka seems to realize for the first time that Sidi has paid no attention to his explanation. She is, in fact, still humming and shaking her shoulders. He stares questioningly at her. Sidi stops, somewhat confused and embarrassed, points sheepishly to the wrestler.*]

SIDI: I think this time he will win.
[*Baroka's grumbling subsides slowly. He is now attentive to the present bout.*]

BAROKA: Now let us once again take up
The questioning. [*Almost timidly.*] Is this man
Good and kindly.

SIDI: They say he uses well
His dogs and horses.

BAROKA: [*desperately.*]
Well is he fierce then? Reckless!
Does the bush cow run to hole
When he hears his beaters' Hei-ei-wo-rah!

SIDI: There are heads and skins of leopards
Hung around his council room.
But the market is also
Full of them.

BAROKA: Is he not wise? Is he not sagely?
Do the young and old not seek
His counsel?

SIDI: The Fox is said to be wise
So cunning that he stalks and dines on
New-hatched chickens.

BAROKA: [*more and more desperate.*]
Does he not beget strength on wombs?
Are his children not tall and stout-limbed?

SIDI: Once upon a time.

BAROKA: Once upon a time?
What do you mean, girl?

SIDI: Just once upon a time.
Perhaps his children have of late
Been plagued with shyness and refuse
To come into the world. Or else
He is so tired with the day's affairs
That at night, he turns his buttocks
To his wives. But there have been
No new reeds cut by his servants,
No new cots woven.
And his household gods are starved
For want of child-naming festivities
Since the last two rains went by.

BAROKA: Perhaps he is a frugal man.
Mindful of years to come,

Planning for a final burst of life, he
Husbands his strength.

SIDI: [*giggling. She is actually stopped, half-way, by giggling at the cleverness of her remark.*]
To husband his wives surely ought to be
A man's first duties—at all times.

BAROKA: My beard tells me you've been a pupil,
A most diligent pupil of Sadiku.
Among all shameless women,
The sharpest tongues grow from that one
Peeling bark—Sadiku, my faithful lizard!
[*Growing steadily warmer during this speech, he again slaps down his opponent's arm as he shouts 'Sadiku'.*]

SIDI: [*backing away, aware that she has perhaps gone too far and betrayed knowledge of the 'secret'.*]
I have learnt nothing of anyone.

BAROKA: No more. No more.
Already I have lost a wrestler
On your account. This town-bred daring
Of little girls, awakes in me
A seven-horned devil of strength.
Let one woman speak a careless word
And I can pin a wriggling—Bah!
[*Lets go the man's arm. He has risen during the last speech but held on to the man's arm, who is forced to rise with him.*]
The tappers should have called by now.
See if we have a fresh gourd by the door.
[*The wrestler goes out. Baroka goes to sit on the bed, Sidi eyeing him, doubtfully.*]
What an ill-tempered man I daily grow
Towards. Soon my voice will be
The sand between two grinding stones.
But I have my scattered kindliness
Though few occasions serve to herald it.

And Sidi, my daughter, you do not know
The thoughts which prompted me
To ask the pleasure that I be your host
This evening, I would not tell Sadiku,
Meaning to give delight
With the surprise of it. Now, tell me, child
Can you guess a little at this thing?

SIDI: Sadiku told me nothing.

BAROKA: You are hasty with denial. For how indeed
Could Sadiku, since I told her
Nothing of my mind, But, my daughter,
Did she not, perhaps . . . invent some tale?
For I know Sadiku loves to be
All-knowing.

SIDI: She said no more, except the Bale
Begged my presence.

BAROKA: [*rises quickly to the bait.*]
Begged? Bale Baroka begged?
[*Wrestler enters with gourd and calabash-cups. Baroka relapses.*]
Ah! I see you love to bait your elders.
One way the world remains the same,
The child still thinks she is wiser than
The cotton head of age.
Do you think Baroka deaf or blind
To little signs? But let that pass.
Only, lest you fall victim to the schemes
Of busy women, I will tell you this—
I know Sadiku plays the match-maker
Without the prompting. If I look
On any maid, or call her name
Even in the course of harmless, neighbourly
Well-wishing—How fares your daughter?
—Is your sister now recovered from her

Whooping cough?—How fast your ward
Approaches womanhood! Have the village lads
Begun to gather at your door?—
Or any word at all which shows I am
The thoughtful guardian of the village health,
If it concerns a woman, Sadiku straightway
Flings herself into the role of go-between
And before I even don a cap, I find
Yet another stranger in my bed!

SIDI: It seems a Bale's life
Is full of great unhappiness.

BAROKA: I do not complain. No, my child
I accept the sweet and sour with
A ruler's grace. I lose my patience
Only when I meet with
The new immodesty with women.
Now, my Sidi, you have not caught
This new and strange disease, I hope.

SIDI: [*curtsying.*] The threading of my smock—
Does Baroka not know the marking
Of the village loom?

BAROKA: But will Sidi, the pride of mothers,
Will she always wear it?

SIDI: Will Sidi, the proud daughter of Baroka,
Will she step out naked?
[*A pause. Baroka surveys Sidi in an almost fatherly manner and she bashfully drops her eyes.*]

BAROKA: To think that once I thought,
Sidi is the eye's delight, but
She is vain, and her head
Is feather-light, and always giddy
With a trivial thought. And now
I find her deep and wise beyond her years.
[*Reaches under his pillow, brings out the now familiar*

magazine, and also an addressed envelope. Retains the former and gives her the envelope.]
Do you know what this means?
The trim red piece of paper
In the corner?

SIDI: I know it. A stamp. Lakunle receives
Letters from Lagos marked with it.

BAROKA: [*obviously disappointed.*]
Hm. Lakunle. But more about him
Later. Do you know what it means—
This little frippery?

SIDI: [*very proudly.*]
Yes. I know that too. Is it not a tax on
The habit of talking with paper?

BAROKA: Oh. Oh. I see you dip your hand
Into the pockets of the school teacher
And retrieve it bulging with knowledge.
[*Goes to the strange machine, and pulls the lever up and down.*]
Now this, not even the school teacher can tell
What magic this performs. Come nearer,
It will not bite.

SIDI: I have never seen the like.

BAROKA: The work dear child, of the palace blacksmiths
Built in full secrecy. All is not well with it—
But I will find the cause and then Ilujinle
Will boast its own tax on paper, made with
Stamps like this. For long I dreamt it
And here it stands, child of my thoughts.

SIDI: [*wonder-struck.*] You mean . . . this will work some day?

BAROKA: Ogun has said the word. And now my girl
What think you of that image on the stamp
This spiderwork of iron, wood and mortar?

SIDI: Is it not a bridge?

BAROKA: It is a bridge. The longest—so they say

In the whole country. When not a bridge,
You'll find a print of groundnuts
Stacked like pyramids,
Or palm trees, or cocoa-trees, and farmers
Hacking pods, and workmen
Felling trees and tying skinned logs
Into rafts. A thousand thousand letters
By road, by rail, by air,
From one end of the world to another,
And not one human head among them;
Not one head of beauty on the stamp?

SIDI: But I once saw Lakunle's letter
With a head of bronze.

BAROKA: A figurehead, my child, a lifeless work
Of craft, with holes for eyes, and coldness
For the warmth of life and love
In youthful cheeks like yours,
My daughter . . .
[*Pauses to watch the effect on Sidi.*]
. . . Can you see it, Sidi?
Tens of thousands of these dainty prints
And each one with this legend of Sidi.
[*Flourishes the magazine, open in the middle.*]
The village goddess, reaching out
Towards the sun, her lover.
Can you see it, my daughter!
[*Sidi drowns herself totally in the contemplation, takes the magazine but does not even look at it. Sits on the bed.*]

BAROKA: [*very gently.*]
I hope you will not think it too great
A burden, to carry the country's mail
All on your comeliness.
[*Walks away, an almost business-like tone.*]
Our beginnings will

Of course be modest. We shall begin
By cutting stamps for our own village alone.
As the schoolmaster himself would say—
Charity begins at home.
[*Pause. Faces Sidi from nearly the distance of the room.*]
For a long time now,
The town-dwellers have made up tales
Of the backwardness of Ilujinle
Until it hurts Baroka, who holds
The welfare of his people deep at heart.
Now, if we do this thing, it will prove more
Than any single town has done!
[*The wrestler, who has been listening open-mouthed, drops his cup in admiration. Baroka, annoyed, realizing only now in fact that he is still in the room, waves him impatiently out.*]
I do not hate progress, only its nature
Which makes all roofs and faces look the same.
And the wish of one old man is
That here and there,
[*Goes progressively towards Sidi, until he bends over her, then sits beside her on the bed.*]
Among the bridges and the murderous roads,
Below the humming birds which
Smoke the face of Sango, dispenser of
The snake-tongue lightning; between this moment
And the reckless broom that will be wielded
In these years to come, we must leave
Virgin plots of lives, rich decay
And the tang of vapour rising from
Forgotten heaps of compost, lying
Undisturbed . . . But the skin of progress
Masks, unknown, the spotted wolf of sameness . . .
Does sameness not revolt your being,
My daughter?

[*Sidi is capable only of a bewildered nod, slowly.*]

BAROKA: [*sighs, hands folded piously on his lap.*]
I find my soul is sensitive, like yours,
Indeed, although there is one—no more think I—
One generation between yours and mine,
Our thoughts fly crisply through the air
And meet, purified, as one.
And our first union
Is the making of this stamp.
The one redeeming grace on any paper-tax
Shall be your face. And mine,
The soul behind it all, worshipful
Of Nature for her gift of youth
And beauty to our earth. Does this
Please you, my daughter?

SIDI: I can no longer see the meaning, Baroka.
Now that you speak
Almost like the school teacher, except
Your words fly on a different path,
I find . . .

BAROKA: It is a bad thing, then, to sound
Like your school teacher?

SIDI: No Bale, but words are like beetles
Boring at my ears, and my head
Becomes a jumping bean. Perhaps after all,
As the school teacher tells me often,
[*Very miserably.*]
I have a simple mind.

BAROKA: [*pats her kindly on the head.*]
No, Sidi, not simple, only straight and truthful
Like a fresh-water reed. But I do find
Your school teacher and I are much alike.
The proof of wisdom is the wish to learn
Even from children. And the haste of youth

Must learn its temper from the gloss
Of ancient leather, from a strength
Knit close along the grain. The school teacher
And I, must learn one from the other.
Is this not right?
[*A tearful nod.*]

BAROKA: The old must flow into the new, Sidi,
Not blind itself or stand foolishly
Apart. A girl like you must inherit
Miracles which age alone reveals.
Is this not so?

SIDI: Everything you say, Bale,
Seems wise to me.

BAROKA: Yesterday's wine alone is strong and blooded, child,
And though the Christians' holy book denies
The truth of this, old wine thrives best
Within a new bottle. The coarseness
Is mellowed down, and the rugged wine
Acquires a full and rounded body . . .
Is this not so—my child?
[*Quite overcome, Sidi nods.*]

BAROKA: Those who know little of Baroka think
His life one pleasure-living course.
But the monkey sweats, my child,
The monkey sweats,
It is only the hair upon his back
Which still deceives the world . . .
[*Sidi's head falls slowly on the Bale's shoulder. The Bale remains in his final body-weighed-down-by-burdens-of-State attitude.*
Even before the scene is completely shut off a crowd of dancers burst in at the front and dance off at the opposite side without slackening pace. In their brief appearance it should be apparent that they comprise a group of female dancers pursuing a

masked male. Drumming and shouts continue quite audibly and shortly afterwards. They enter and re-cross the stage in the same manner.
The shouts fade away and they next appear at the market clearing. It is now full evening. Lakunle and Sadiku are still waiting for Sidi's return. The traders are beginning to assemble one by one, ready for the evening market. Hawkers pass through with oil-lamps beside their ware. Food sellers enter with cooking-pots and foodstuffs, set up their 'adogan' or stone hearth and build a fire.
All this while, Lakunle is pacing wretchedly, Sadiku looks on placidly.]

LAKUNLE: [*he is pacing furiously.*]
He's killed her.
I warned you. You know him,
And I warned you.
[*Goes up all the approaches to look.*]
She's been gone half the day. It will soon
Be daylight. And still no news.
Women have disappeared before.
No trace. Vanished. Now we know how.
[*Checks, turns round.*]
And why!
Mock an old man, will you? So?
You can laugh? Ha ha! You wait.
I'll come and see you
Whipped like a dog. Baroka's head wife
Driven out of the house for plotting
With a girl.
[*Each approaching footstep brings Lakunle to attention, but it is only a hawker or a passer-by. The wrestler passes. Sadiku greets him familiarly. Then, after he has passed, some significance of this breaks on Sadiku and she begins to look a little puzzled.*]

LAKUNLE: I know he has dungeons. Secret holes
Where a helpless girl will lie
And rot for ever. But not for nothing
Was I born a man. I'll find my way
To rescue her. She little deserves it, but
I shall risk my life for her.
[*The mummers can now be heard again, distantly. Sadiku and Lakunle become attentive as the noise approaches, Lakunle increasingly uneasy. A little, but not too much notice is paid by the market people.*]
What is that?

SADIKU: If my guess is right, it will be mummers.
[*Adds slyly.*]
Somebody must have told them the news.

LAKUNLE: What news?
[*Sadiku chuckles darkly and comprehension breaks on the School teacher.*]
Baroka! You dared . . . ?
Woman, is there no mercy in your veins?
He gave you children, and he stood
Faithfully by you and them.
He risked his life that you may boast
A warrior-hunter for your lord . . . But you—
You sell him to the rhyming rabble
Gloating in your disloyalty . . .

SADIKU: [*calmly dips her hand in his pocket.*]
Have you any money?

LAKUNLE: [*snatching out her hand.*]
Why? What? . . . Keep away, witch! Have you
Turned pickpocket in your dotage?

SADIKU: Don't be a miser. Will you let them go without giving you a special performance?

LAKUNLE: If you think I care for their obscenity . . .

SADIKU: [*wheedling.*] Come on, school teacher. They'll expect it of you . . . The man of learning . . . the young sprig of foreign wisdom . . . You must not demean yourself in their eyes . . . you must give them money to perform for your lordship . . .

[*Re-enter the mummers, dancing straight through (more centrally this time) as before. Male dancer enters first, pursued by a number of young women and other choral idlers. The man dances in tortured movements. He and about half of his pursuers have already danced off-stage on the opposite side when Sadiku dips her hand briskly in Lakunle's pocket, this time with greater success. Before Lakunle can stop her, she has darted to the drummers and pressed a coin apiece on their foreheads, waving them to possession of the floor. Tilting their heads backwards, they drum her praises. Sadiku denies the credit, points to Lakunle as the generous benefactor. They transfer their attention to him where he stands biting his lips at the trick. The other dancers have now been brought back and the drummers resume the beat of the interrupted dance. The treasurer removes the coins from their foreheads and places them in a pouch. Now begins the dance of virility which is of course none other than the Baroka story. Very athletic movements. Even in his prime, 'Baroka' is made a comic figure, held in a kind of tolerant respect by his women. At his decline and final downfall, they are most unsparing in their taunts and tantalizing motions. Sadiku has never stopped bouncing on her toes through the dance, now she is done the honour of being invited to join at the kill. A dumb show of bashful refusals, then she joins them, reveals surprising agility for her age, to the wild enthusiasm of the rest who surround and spur her on.*

With 'Baroka' finally scotched, the crowd dances away to their incoming movement, leaving Sadiku to dance on oblivious of their departure. The drumming becomes more distant and she unwraps her eyelids. Sighs, looks around her and walks contentedly towards Lakunle. As usual he has enjoyed the spectacle in spite of himself, showing especial relish where 'Baroka' gets the worst of it from his women. Sadiku looks at him for a moment while he tries to replace his obvious enjoyment with disdain. She shouts 'Boo' at him, and breaks into a dance movement, shakes a sudden leg at Lakunle.]

SADIKU: Sadiku of the duiker's feet . . . that's what the men used to call me. I could twist and untwist my waist with the smoothness of a water snake . . .

LAKUNLE: No doubt. And you are still just as slippery.
I hope Baroka kills you for this.
When he finds out what your wagging tongue
Has done to him, I hope he beats you
Till you choke on your own breath . . .
[*Sidi bursts in, she has been running all the way. She throws herself on the ground against the tree and sobs violently, beating herself on the ground.*]

SADIKU: [*on her knees beside her.*] Why, child. What is the matter?

SIDI: [*pushes her off.*]
Get away from me. Do not touch me.

LAKUNLE: [*with a triumphant smile, he pulls Sadiku away and takes her place.*]
Oh, Sidi, let me kiss your tears . . .

SIDI: [*pushes him so hard that he sits down abruptly.*]
Don't touch me.

LAKUNLE: [*dusting himself.*]
He must have beaten her.
Did I not warn you both?
Baroka is a creature of the wilds,
Untutored, mannerless, devoid of grace.
[*Sidi only cries all the more, beats on the ground with clenched fists and stubs her toes in the ground.*]
Chief though he is,
I shall kill him for this . . .
No. Better still, I shall demand
Redress from the central courts.
I shall make him spend
The remainder of his wretched life

In prison—with hard labour.
I'll teach him
To beat defenceless women . . .

SIDI: [*lifting her head.*]
Fool! You little fools! It was a lie.
The frog. The cunning frog!
He lied to you, Sadiku.

SADIKU: Sango forbid!

SIDI: He told me . . . afterwards, crowing.
It was a trick.
He knew Sadiku would not keep it to herself,
That I, or maybe other maids would hear of it
And go to mock his plight.
And how he laughed!
How his frog-face croaked and croaked
And called me little fool!
Oh how I hate him! How I loathe
And long to kill the man!

LAKUNLE: [*retreating.*] But Sidi, did he . . . ? I mean . . .
Did you escape?
[*Louder sobs from Sidi.*]
Speak, Sidi, this is agony.
Tell me the worst; I'll take it like a man.
Is it the fright which effects you so,
Or did he . . . ? Sidi, I cannot bear the thought.
The words refuse to form.
Do not unman me, Sidi. Speak
Before I burst in tears.

SADIKU: [*raises Sidi's chin in her hand.*]
Sidi, are you a maid or not?
[*Sidi shakes her head violently and bursts afresh in tears.*]

LAKUNLE: The Lord forbid!

SADIKU: Too late for prayers. Cheer up. It happens to the best of us.

LAKUNLE: Oh heavens, strike me dead!
Earth, open up and swallow Lakunle.
For he no longer has the wish to live.
Let the lightning fall and shrivel me
To dust and ashes . . .
[*Recoils.*]
No, that wish is cowardly. This trial is my own.
Let Sango and his lightning keep out of this. It
Is my cross, and let it not be spoken that
In the hour of need, Lakunle stood
Upon the scales and was proved wanting.
My love is selfless—the love of spirit
Not of flesh.
[*Stands over Sidi.*]
Dear Sidi, we shall forget the past.
This great misfortune touches not
The treasury of my love.
But you will agree, it is only fair
That we forget the bride-price totally
Since you no longer can be called a maid.
Here is my hand; if on these terms,
You'll be my cherished wife.
We'll take an oath, between us three
That this shall stay
A secret to our dying days . . .
[*Takes a look at Sadiku and adds quickly.*]
Oh no, a secret even after we're dead and gone.
And if Baroka dares to boast of it,
I'll swear he is a liar—and swear by Sango too!
[*Sidi raises herself slowly, staring at Lakunle with unbelieving eyes. She is unsmiling, her face a puzzle.*]

SIDI: You would? You would marry me?

LAKUNLE: [*puffs out his chest.*] Yes.
[*Without a change of expression, Sidi dashes suddenly off the stage.*]

SADIKU: What on earth has got into her?

LAKUNLE: I wish I knew
She took off suddenly
Like a hunted buck.
[*Looks off-stage.*]
I think—yes, she is,
She is going home.
Sadiku, will you go?
Find out if you can
What she plans to do.
[*Sadiku nods and goes. Lakunle walks up and down.*]
And now I know I am the biggest fool
That ever walked this earth.
There are women to be found
In every town or village in these parts,
And every one a virgin.
But I obey my books.
[*Distant music. Light drums, flutes, box-guitars, 'sekere'.*]
'Man takes the fallen woman by the hand'
And ever after they live happily.
Moreover, I will admit,
It solves the problem of her bride-price too.
A man must live or fall by his true
Principles. That, I had sworn,
Never to pay.
[*Enter Sadiku.*]

SADIKU: She is packing her things. She is gathering her clothes and trinkets together, and oiling herself as a bride does before her wedding.

LAKUNLE: Heaven help us! I am not impatient.
Surely she can wait a day or two at least.
There is the asking to be done,
And then I have to hire a praise-singer,
And such a number of ceremonies

Must firstly be performed.

SADIKU: Just what I said but she only laughed at me and called me a . . . a . . . what was it now . . . a bra . . . braba . . . brabararian. It serves you right. It all comes of your teaching. I said what about the asking and the other ceremonies. And she looked at me and said, leave all that nonsense to savages and brabararians.

LAKUNLE: But I must prepare myself.
I cannot be
A single man one day and a married one the next.
It must come gradually.
I will not wed in haste.
A man must have time to prepare,
To learn to like the thought.
I must think of my pupils too:
Would they be pleased if I were married
Not asking their consent . . . ?
[*The singing group is now audible even to him.*]
What is that? The musicians?
Could they have learnt so soon?

SADIKU: The news of a festivity travels fast. You ought to know that.

LAKUNLE: The goddess of malicious gossip
Herself must have a hand in my undoing.
The very spirits of the partial air
Have all conspired to blow me, willy-nilly
Down the slippery slope of grim matrimony.
What evil have I done . . . ? Ah, here they come!
[*Enter crowd and musicians.*]
Go back. You are not needed yet. Nor ever.
Hence parasites, you've made a big mistake.
There is no one getting wedded; get you home.
[*Sidi now enters. In one hand she holds a bundle, done up in a richly embroidered cloth: in the other the magazine. She is*

radiant, jewelled, lightly clothed, and wears light leather-thong sandals. They all go suddenly silent except for the long-drawn O-Ohs of admiration. She goes up to Lakunle and hands him the book.]

SIDI: A present from Sidi.
I tried to tear it up
But my fingers were too frail.
[*To the crowd.*]
Let us go.
[*To Lakunle.*]
You may come too if you wish,
You are invited.

LAKUNLE: [*lost in the miracle of transformation.*]
Well I should hope so indeed
Since I am to marry you.

SIDI: [*turns round in surprise.*]
Marry who . . . ? You thought . . .
Did you really think that you, and I . . .
Why, did you think that after him,
I could endure the touch of another man?
I who have felt the strength,
The perpetual youthful zest
Of the panther of the trees?
And would I choose a watered-down,
A beardless version of unripened man?

LAKUNLE: [*bars her way.*]
I shall not let you.
I shall protect you from yourself.

SIDI: [*gives him a shove that sits him down again, hard against the tree base.*]
Out of my way, book-nourished shrimp.
Do you see what strength he has given me?
That was not bad. For a man of sixty,
It was the secret of God's own draught

A deed for drums and ballads.
But you, at sixty, you'll be ten years dead!
In fact, you'll not survive your honeymoon . . .
Come to my wedding if you will. If not . . .
[*She shrugs her shoulders. Kneels down at Sadiku's feet.*]
Mother of brides, your blessing . . .

SADIKU: [*lays her hand on Sidi's head.*] I invoke the fertile gods.
They will stay with you. May the time come soon when
you shall be as round-bellied as a full moon in a low sky.

SIDI: [*hands her the bundle.*]
Now bless my wordly goods.
[*Turns to the musicians.*]
Come, sing to me of seeds
Of children, sired of the lion stock.
[*The Musicians resume their tune. Sidi sings and dances.*]
Mo te'ni. Mo te'ni.
Mo te'ni. Mo te'ni.
Sun mo mi, we mo mi
Sun mo mi, fa mo mi
Yarabi lo m'eyi t'o le d'omo . . .

[*Festive air, fully pervasive. Oil lamps from the market multiply as traders desert their stalls to join them. A young girl flaunts her dancing buttocks at Lakunle and he rises to the bait. Sadiku gets in his way as he gives chase. Tries to make him dance with her. Lakunle last seen, having freed himself of Sadiku, clearing a space in the crowd for the young girl.*
The crowd repeat the song after Sidi.]

Tolani Tolani
T'emi ni T'emi ni
Sun mo mi, we mo mi
Sun mo mi, fa mo mi
Yarabi lo m'eyi t'o le d'omo.

'In that richly ribald comedy, *The Lion and the Jewel*, poetry and prose are also blended, but with a marvellous lightness in the treatment of both. The big set-piece of miming in the opening scene, where the villagers re-enact the visit of the white photographer, and the seduction of the village jewel Sidi by the old Lion of a chief, are two of the pinnacles of Mr. Soyinka's achievement to date.' *The Times Literary Supplement.*

'The contemporary theater seems to have forgotten that it has its roots in ritual and song, and it is only the rare emergence of a Lorca or a Brecht—or a Wole Soyinka—that recreates an awareness of our deprivation.' *African Forum.*

'. . . a brilliant dramatist—the most important in Nigeria, if not in all Black Africa. He is helped by a profound command of the English language, reflected sometimes in the dazzling brilliance, at other times in the intense poetic quality of his writing . . .' *West Africa.*

'He does not use the culture of his ancestors as a gimmick to sell his abilities or even as an export commodity, but as inborn material for expansion. His skilful use of idiom with the lively and musical Nigerian flavour in no way detracts from the command of the English language which he possesses.' *Times Educational Supplement.*

The Times, at the time of its production at the Royal Court Theatre, London in December 1966, said:
'This is the third play by Wole Soyinka to appear in London since last year, and this work alone is enough to establish Nigeria as the most fertile new source of English-speaking drama since Synge's discovery of the Western Isles . . . Even this comparison does Soyinka less than justice, for he is dealing not only with rich folk material, but with the impact of the modern on tribal custom: to find any parallel for his work in English drama you have to go back to the Elizabethans.'

Nobel Laureate